100 "Mate in 3" Chess Puzzles for Advanced Players (Rating 1500-1800)

100 real-life chess tactics puzzles for advanced players

D0924557

100 "Mate in 3" Chess Puzzles for Advanced Players (Rating 1500-1800)

Published by www.chess-books.co.uk

ISBN: 978-1-78933-255-1

Copyright © 2021 The Chess Puzzler

Cover Image Copyright: Shutterstock

Table of Contents

Introduction

Hi! I'm the Chess Puzzler and I'm here to make you a better chess player.

Chess puzzles are an essential part of your development as a player and contribute a massively to your tactical understanding of the game. Even Grandmasters devote time every day to solving chess puzzles to keep them sharp and improve their chess "intuition".

Right from the opening and on into the middle and end game, strong chess players always have an eye out for "tactics" and will quickly recognize positions on the board that are similar to positions they have studied in practice. Building this intuition quickly helps you spot unexpected *smiting* moves and longer combinations that your opponent hasn't seen. They will save you time on the board by teaching you where to look, and help build the kind of vision that will make your rating skyrocket.

However, a word of caution! While solving chess puzzles will absolutely improve your calculation and strategy skills, you need to also develop a feel for *when* to start calculating in a real game because most games you play will begin with a *quiet* position. For that reason, you should concurrently develop your understanding of *positional* chess which breaks down into building strong openings and knowing how to develop your pieces so that they work together on the board. Studying chess tactics is essential, but knowing when to start looking for them in an actual game is an important skill too, otherwise you'll just run out your clock.

As a rule of thumb, you should spend more time calculating tactics in a game when there is *tension* on the board. Often (but of course, not exclusively) this is when the opening is complete and opposing pieces are starting to come into contact.

The types of puzzles that will improve your game most quickly are the ones that have been played by real people (every puzzle in this book has been), and you should steer away from complicated imaginary positions that wouldn't appear in a real game. They can be fun, but you want to focus on real life situations. It's all about building that chess intuition!

Get Free Chess Puzzles

If you want to get better quickly, you can download our free intermediate book of 300 mixed chess puzzles from:

www.chess-books.co.uk/free

or by scanning this QR code with your smart phone

You'll get 300 mixed chess puzzles that start from beginner and move right through to fiendish levels!

All you need to do is fill in the form and we'll email you your book immediately.

Download it now!

The Puzzles

Ready to dive in?

The chess puzzles in this book are all taken from real-life games and are solved by checkmating your opponent in three moves.

The solutions are written on the back of each page for easy reference - so no peaking!

The best way to train your brain is to solve the puzzle in its entirety before looking at any part of the solution.

For best results:

Set up the position on a physical chess board and give yourself 10 minutes to explore the first three strongest looking candidate moves. These include moves that *force* a response from your opponent, such as checks or the potential capture of an undefended piece.

For each move, explore the opponent's possible responses and then calculate what subsequent move would be strongest for you in return. This should lead you towards the solution.

Spend more time exploring the moves that look to give a more positive outcome, but don't forget that the best moves aren't always the most intuitive ones – at least not yet!

If none of your initial moves offer an immediately positive outcome, then look for a positional move that help develop your pieces to a point where you have an advantage or subsequent forcing move.

Remember that forks, skewers, decoys, double attacks, and mating patterns are all things you should be looking out for when learning to solve chess puzzles.

1 - Black to Move

2 - Black to Move

3 - Black to Move

4 - White to Move

Solutions

1) 1... Rb1+ 2. Kxb1 Qb3+ 3. Ka1 Qb2#

2) 1... Qg1+ 2. Rf1 Qxe3+ 3. Kd1 Qd2#

3) 1... Bg2+ 2. Rxg2 Rh3+ 3. Rh2 Rxh2#

4) 1. Qf7+ Kh8 2. Qxf8+ Rxf8 3. Rxf8#

5 - Black to Move

6 - White to Move

7 - Black to Move

8 - White to Move

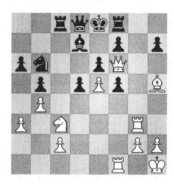

Solutions

5)   1... R8a2+ 2. Kc3 Rc1+ 3. Bc2 Rcxc2#

6)   1. Nxc7+ Qxc7 2. Qxf7+ Kd8 3. Ne6#

7)   1... Qd2+ 2. Kb1 Qd1+ 3. Rxd1 Rxd1#

8)   1. Bxf7+ Rxf7 2. Rg8+ Rf8 3. Rxf8#

9 - Black to Move

10 - White to Move

11 - Black to Move

12 - Black to Move

Solutions

9) 1... Qxf2+ 2. Kh1 Qf1+ 3. Ng1 Nf2#

10) 1. Rd8+ Rc8 2. Rxc8+ Qxc8 3. Rxc8#

11) 1... Kh8 2. Rf2 Rh5+ 3. Rh2 Rxh2#

12) 1... Bh2+ 2. Kh1 Bg1+ 3. Kxg1 Qh2#

13 - Black to Move

14 - Black to Move

15 - White to Move

16 - Black to Move

Solutions

13) 1... Rxe1+ 2. Rf1 Rxf1+ 3. Bxf1 Qxf1#

14) 1... Qa2+ 2. Kc1 Qa1+ 3. Kd2 Qxb2#

15) 1. Qa8+ Qf8 2. Be6+ Kh8 3. Qxf8#

16) 1... hxg2+ 2. Kxg2 Qh2+ 3. Kf1 Qf2#

17 - Black to Move

18 - Black to Move

19 - Black to Move

20 - Black to Move

Solutions

17) 1... Qxd1+ 2. Qxd1 Rc1+ 3. Qxc1 Rxc1#

18) 1... Nh3+ 2. Kh1 Qg1+ 3. Rxg1 Nf2#

19) 1... Nh3+ 2. Kh1 Qg1+ 3. Rxg1 Nf2#

20) 1... Qxf2+ 2. Kh1 Qg1+ 3. Rxg1 Nf2#

21 - Black to Move

22 - White to Move

23 - Black to Move

24 - Black to Move

Solutions

21) 1... Nf3+ 2. gxf3 Rg5+ 3. Kh1 Qxf3#

22) 1. Rg8+ Rxg8 2. Rxg8+ Rxg8 3. fxg8=Q#

23) 1... Rxe4+ 2. Kf1 Qxa1+ 3. Ne1 Qxe1#

24) 1... Rd1+ 2. Bxd1 Qxf2+ 3. Kh1 Qxg2#

25 - White to Move

26 - Black to Move

27 - White to Move

28 - Black to Move

Solutions

25) 1. e5+ f5 2. exf6+ Kh8 3. Qxh6#

26) 1... Rxg8+ 2. Kh1 Bg2+ 3. Kg1 Bf3#

27) 1. Rxf8+ Rxf8 2. Rxf8+ Qg8 3. Nf7#

28) 1... Qxb3+ 2. Ka1 Rxc1+ 3. Rxc1 Qb2#

29 - White to Move

30 - White to Move

31 - Black to Move

32 - White to Move

Solutions

29) 1. Nc6+ Ka8 2. Rxb8+ Rxb8 3. Rxb8#

30) 1. Qg6+ Kh8 2. Qxh6+ Rh7 3. Qxf8#

31) 1... Ne3+ 2. Kh1 Be4+ 3. f3 Bxf3#

32) 1. Qxb8+ Qd8 2. Re8+ Qxe8 3. Qxe8#

33 - White to Move

34 - Black to Move

35 - Black to Move

36 - White to Move

Solutions

33) 1. Na6+ Rxa6+ 2. bxa6 g3 3. a7#

34) 1... Kg3 2. Rxf5 Re1+ 3. Rf1 Rxf1#

35) 1... Rd1+ 2. Qc1 Bxa2+ 3. Ka1 Rxc1#

36) 1. Kg6 Re3 2. Rc8+ Re8 3. Rxe8#

37 - White to Move

38 - White to Move

39 - Black to Move

40 - Black to Move

Solutions

37) 1. Qxd8+ Rxd8 2. Re8+ Rxe8 3. fxe8=Q#

38) 1. Rh4+ Bh6 2. Rxh6+ Kg7 3. Rh7#

39) 1... Qxf2+ 2. Kh1 Qf1+ 3. Rxf1 Rxf1#

40) 1... Rxb1+ 2. Rxb1 Rxb1+ 3. Kxb1 Qb2#

41 - White to Move

42 - Black to Move

43 - White to Move

44 - White to Move

Solutions

41) 1. Rxe8+ Kxe8 2. Qc8+ Bd8 3. Qxc6#

42) 1... Ng3+ 2. Kxh2 Nf1+ 3. Kg1 Qh2#

43) 1. Rxh4+ gxh4 2. Rh5+ Qh7 3. Rxh7#

44) 1. Qa8+ Kd7 2. Qxb7+ Ke8 3. Qe7#

45 - Black to Move

46 - White to Move

47 - White to Move

48 - Black to Move

Solutions

45) 1... Nf3+ 2. Bxf3 Qxf1+ 3. Kd2 Bh6#

46) 1. Rxh6+ gxh6 2. g7+ Kh7 3. g8=Q#

47) 1. Rd8+ Re8 2. Qh6+ Ke7 3. Qd6#

48) 1... Re7+ 2. Kf1 Rd1+ 3. Rxd1 cxd1=Q#

49 - White to Move

50 - Black to Move

51 - Black to Move

52 - White to Move

Solutions

49) 1. Rxb8+ Rxb8 2. Rxb8+ Kxb8 3. Qb7#

50) 1... Qf1+ 2. Kh4 g5+ 3. Kh5 Qh3#

51) 1... Re2+ 2. Kd3 e4+ 3. Kc3 Rc2#

52) 1. exf7+ Kh8 2. Bxg7+ Kxg7 3. Qf6#

53 - White to Move

54 - White to Move

55 - White to Move

56 - Black to Move

Solutions

53) 1. Qg2 Qe6+ 2. Qg4+ Qxg4+ 3. fxg4#

54) 1. Nf8+ Kg8 2. Qh7+ Kxf8 3. Qh8#

55) 1. Nxf7+ Rxf7 2. Qe8+ Rf8 3. Qxf8#

56) 1... Qxh3+ 2. gxh3 g2+ 3. Kh2 g1=Q#

57 - White to Move

58 - Black to Move

59 - Black to Move

60 - Black to Move

Solutions

57) 1. Qg7+ Rxg7 2. hxg7+ Kg8 3. Rh8#

58) 1... Qc1+ 2. Rd1 Bc3+ 3. Nd2 Bxd2#

59) 1... Rxh2+ 2. Kg1 Rh1+ 3. Kg2 R8h2#

60) 1... exd3+ 2. Nd4 Qxd4+ 3. Be3 Qxe3#

61 - Black to Move

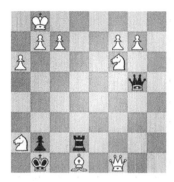

62 - White to Move

63 - Black to Move

64 - White to Move

Solutions

61) 1... Re1+ 2. Kh2 Qf4+ 3. g3 Qxf2#

62) 1. Qb3+ Nd5 2. Qxd5+ Kf8 3. Qf7#

63) 1... Qb2+ 2. Nxb2 cxb2+ 3. Kb1 Rxc1#

64) 1. Ne6+ Kh6 2. Rh2+ Rh4 3. Rxh4#

65 - Black to Move

66 - White to Move

67 - Black to Move

68 - White to Move

Solutions

65) 1... Qxg1+ 2. Kxg1 Rd1+ 3. Qe1 Rxe1#

66) 1. Qxc7+ Ka8 2. Qc8+ Rxc8 3. Rxc8#

67) 1... Qxh2+ 2. Kxh2 Rh6+ 3. Qh4 Rxh4#

68) 1. Kxc6 d1=Q 2. Rh8+ Qd8 3. Rxd8#

69 - White to Move

70 - White to Move

71 - White to Move

72 - White to Move

Solutions

69) 1. Rh8+ Kxh8 2. Qh6+ Kg8 3. Qxg7#

70) 1. h6 Qf8 2. hxg7+ Bh3+ 3. Rxh3#

71) 1. Qa4+ b5 2. Qxb5+ Bc6 3. Qxc6#

72) 1. g5+ Kxg5 2. Qe7+ Kh6 3. Rh4#

73 - White to Move

74 - White to Move

75 - White to Move

76 - Black to Move

Solutions

73) 1. Rc8+ Kb7 2. Rc7+ Ka6 3. Ra7#

74) 1. Qc5+ Qe7 2. Rxf6+ Kg7 3. Qxe7#

75) 1. Bxf7+ Rxf7 2. Rd8+ Rf8 3. Rxf8#

76) 1... Rb1+ 2. Kxb1 Qxa2+ 3. Kc1 Qa1#

77 - Black to Move

78 - White to Move

79 - White to Move

80 - Black to Move

Solutions

77) 1... Qh6 2. Re1 Qh2+ 3. Kf1 Qxf2#

78) 1. Bxg7+ Nxg7 2. Qxf8+ Bxf8 3. Rxf8#

79) 1. Nf6+ gxf6 2. Qg4+ Kh8 3. Bxf6#

80) 1... Nf2+ 2. Rxf2 Qxd1+ 3. Rf1 Qxf1#

81 - Black to Move

82 - Black to Move

83 - Black to Move

84 - White to Move

Solutions

81) 1... Re1+ 2. Nxe1 Qe2+ 3. Kg1 Qxe1#

82) 1... Qxd1+ 2. Rxd1 Rxd1+ 3. Kxd1 Re1#

83) 1... Rxc1+ 2. Kf2 Rf1+ 3. Kg2 Re2#

84) 1. Rxf7+ Rxf7 2. Qg6+ Kh8 3. Nxf7#

85 - Black to Move

86 - White to Move

87 - Black to Move

88 - White to Move

Solutions

85) 1... g5+ 2. Kh5 Rxh3+ 3. Rh4 Rxh4#

86) 1. Qxa8+ Bd8 2. Qxd8+ Rxd8 3. Rxd8#

87) 1... Rd2+ 2. Kh3 Qf1+ 3. Kh4 Rxh2#

88) 1. Qh8+ Kxh8 2. Bf6+ Kg8 3. Rxe8#

89 - Black to Move

90 - White to Move

91 - White to Move

92 - Black to Move

Solutions

89) 1... Rg2+ 2. Kh5 Rh3+ 3. Kg6 Bf4#

90) 1. Nf6+ Kh8 2. Qg8+ Rxg8 3. Rxg8#

91) 1. Rg7+ Kh8 2. Rh7+ Nxh7 3. Qg7#

92) 1... Rh1+ 2. Kxh1 Qxh3+ 3. Kg1 Qxg2#

93 - Black to Move

94 - White to Move

95 - White to Move

96 - White to Move

Solutions

93) 1... Rg6 2. Rxf3+ Bxf3+ 3. Qg5 Rxg5#

94) 1. Qxh7+ Qxh7 2. f7+ Rg7 3. f8=Q#

95) 1. axb7+ Qxb7 2. Rxa7+ Qxa7 3. Qxa7#

96) 1. Nf6 Bg7 2. Rxg7 h2 3. Rh7#

97 - Black to Move

98 - Black to Move

99 - White to Move

100 - White to Move

Solutions

97) 1... Rxh4+ 2. Qh3 Nf3+ 3. Kh1 Rxh3#

98) 1... Qxc2+ 2. Ka1 Qc1+ 3. Nb1 Nc2#

99) 1. Ng6+ fxg6 2. Rxf8+ Bxf8 3. Qxf8#

100)   1. Ra1 Rb3 2. Ra8+ Rb8 3. Rxb8#

Get Free Chess Puzzles

If you want to get better quickly, you can download our free intermediate book of 300 mixed chess puzzles from:

www.chess-books.co.uk/free

or by scanning this QR code with your smart phone

You'll get 300 mixed chess puzzles that start from beginner and move right through to fiendish levels!

All you need to do is fill in the form and we'll email you your book immediately.

Download it now!

Made in the USA
Las Vegas, NV
07 December 2022

61427380R00036